# LANGUAGE OF THE IMMORTALS

This title is part of a series of books entitled
ESSENTIAL INDIA EDITIONS. Each book in the series will explore a
foundational aspect of the country in new and thought-provoking ways.

~

# LANGUAGE
# OF THE
# IMMORTALS

## A CONCISE STUDY OF SANSKRIT

# G. N. Devy

**ALEPH**

**ALEPH**

ALEPH BOOK COMPANY
An independent publishing firm
promoted by *Rupa Publications India*

First published in India in 2025
by Aleph Book Company
161-B/4, Gulmohar House,
Yusuf Sarai Community Centre,
New Delhi 110049

ISBN: 978-93-6523-543-2

1 3 5 7 9 10 8 6 4 2

*Dedicated to Shrikant Bahulkar*
*Scholar of the Vedas, Sanskrit, and Buddhism par excellence,*
*and a friend*

# CONTENTS

# India in the Vedic Age

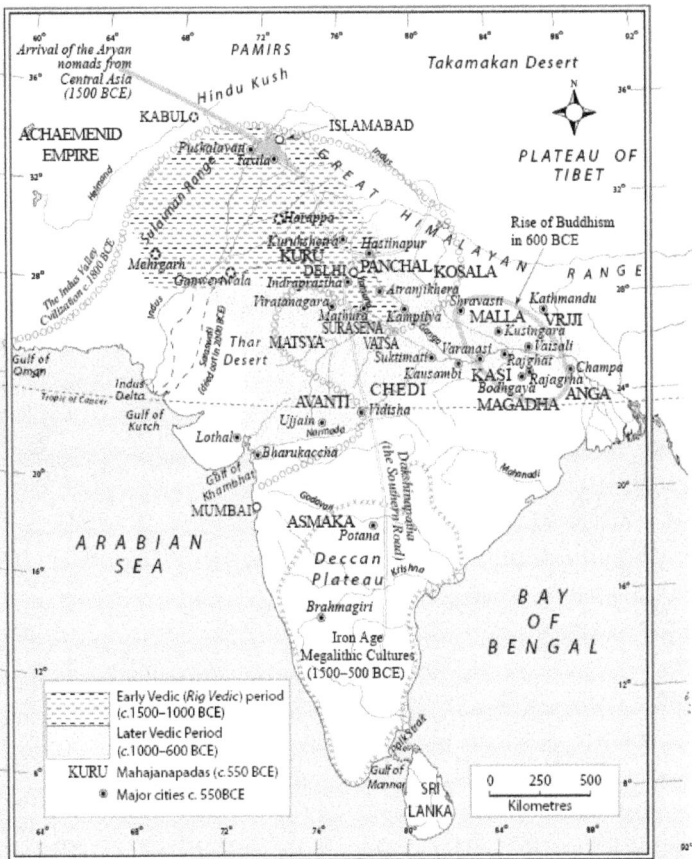

Arrival of the Aryan nomads from Central Asia (1500 BCE)

PAMIRS

Takamakan Desert

Hindu Kush

KABUL

ISLAMABAD

ACHAEMENID EMPIRE

PLATEAU OF TIBET

Pushkalavati
Taxila

GREAT HIMALAYAN RANGE

Salauman Range

Harappa

Rise of Buddhism in 600 BCE

Mehrgarh

Kurukshetra
Hastinapur
KURU
DELHI PANCHAL KOSALA
Ganweriwala Indraprastha
Viratanagara Atranjikhera
Mathura Shravasti Kathmandu
Mathura Kampilya MALLA VRJI
SURASENA Kusingara
Thar MATSYA VATSA Varanasi Vaisali
Desert Suktimati Rajghat Champa
Kausambi KASI Rajagriha
AVANTI CHEDI Bodhgaya ANGA
Ujjain Vidisha MAGADHA
Lothal Narmada
Bharukaccha

The Indus Valley Civilization 2600 BCE

Helmand

Indus

Saraswati (lost river)

Gulf of Oman

Tropic of Cancer

Indus Delta

Gulf of Kutch

Dakshinapatha (the Southern Road)

MUMBAI

Godavari

ASMAKA
Potana

Deccan Plateau

Krishna

Brahmagiri

Iron Age Megalithic Cultures (1500–500 BCE)

ARABIAN SEA

BAY OF BENGAL

Mahanadi

| | Early Vedic (Rig Vedic) period (c.1500–1000 BCE) |
| | Later Vedic Period (c.1000–600 BCE) |
| KURU | Mahajanapadas (c.550 BCE) |
| ● | Major cities c. 550BCE |

Gulf of Mannar

SRI LANKA

0   250   500
Kilometres

Not to scale. This map has been prepared in adherence to the 'Guidelines for acquiring and producing Geospatial Data and Geospatial Data Services including Maps' published vide DST F.No.SM/25/02/2020 (Part-I) dated 15th February, 2021.

# A NOTE FOR READERS

A well-set convention of transliterating Sanskrit words in the Roman script has evolved during the last two centuries. The transliteration convention helps in rendering the original Sanskrit pronunciation with remarkable accuracy. But that transliteration convention involves a far too frequent use of diacritical marks and fixing values of characters—for instance, 'c' for indicating the 'ch' sound—which can elude the common reader's reading comprehension. Therefore, in this book, I have rendered Sanskrit terms into neutral Roman spellings for the ease of reading, despite knowing that the Roman script does not have the full repertoire of characters to accurately capture pronunciations of all consonants and vowels of Sanskrit.

Assigning exact dates to authors and texts from ancient India is a challenging task. It was not usually preferred by ancient authors to claim authorial credit. Besides, it was also a practice to assign the work's origin to an earlier thinker or text. However, thanks to the dedicated textual analysis by numerous scholars during the last century, texts or authors previously difficult to date have been assigned at least some approximate dates. Care is taken in this book to specify the known or assigned lifespan or time period in every single case. Yet, it is necessary to remember that more rigorous research in the future may result in shifting of the dates mentioned in this book.

In recent times, the Sanskrit language has got entangled with active politics and the subject has become invested with high emotions. Objectivity and scientific view of things are the first casualties of a sentimental division of opinion. The present book is written as a scientific and unbiased study of the language. Naturally, therefore, it is not likely to match the sentiments and opinions driven by political biases. If any statement in this book unknowingly offends anyone, I offer apologies in advance to such readers. I would like to hope that Indian readers will display the age-old Indian virtue of tolerance towards a different point of view.

# FALSE PERCEPTION AND MISGUIDED DEBATES

### THE ABIDING INTEREST IN SANSKRIT

Sanskrit is one of the oldest languages in the world. It is also older than most of the other ancient languages such as Arabic, Chinese, Greek, Latin, Hebrew, Pali, Persian, and Tamil. Besides, it has the distinction of being—like Arabic, Hebrew, Latin, and Pali—a language of the scriptures. During the pre-modern centuries, for over a millennium and a half, Sanskrit attracted the attention of the Arabic, Chinese, Greek, Tibetan, and Turkic scholars travelling in India. From the time modern Europe came in contact with India, Sanskrit continued to fascinate generations of Western scholars and linguists. Over the last two and a half centuries, numerous British,

German, French, Dutch, and American scholars of eminence have spent their lives trying to unravel the history of Sanskrit texts and the complexity of thought in them. To name only the most iconic among them: Sir William Jones (1746–94), Henry Thomas Colebrooke (1765–1837), August von Schlegel (1767–1845), H. H. Wilson (1786–1860), William Dwight Whitney (1827–94), Georg Bühler (1837–98), Arthur Macdonell (1854–1930), Monier Monier-Williams (1819–99), Friedrich Max Müller (1823–1900), Arthur Berriedale Keith (1879–1944), Jan Gonda (1905–91), Louis Renou (1896–1966), H. H. Hock (b. 1938), Thomas Trautmann (b. 1940), Michael Witzel (b. 1943), and David Shulman (b. 1949).

Within South Asia too, a series of most illustrious scholars have devoted their lives for the past two centuries to enrich the world's knowledge of Sanskrit, its literature, and its thought. These, again to name only some, include, R. G. Bhandarkar (1837–1925), M. Hiriyanna (1871–1950), Sri Aurobindo (1872–1950), Ananda K. Coomaraswamy (1877–1947), P. V. Kane (1880–1972), Gopinath Kaviraj (1887–1976), Benimadhab Barua (1888–1948), Rahul Sankrityayan (1893–1963),

Prabodh Chandra Bagchi (1898–1956), R. N. Dandekar (1909–2001), K. Krishnamoorthy (1923–97), Ramaranjan Mukherji (1928–2010), and B. K. Matilal (1935–91). The creative writers and philosophers in numerous languages outside India—Johann Wolfgang von Goethe (1749–1832), Arthur Schopenhauer (1788–1860), Friedrich Nietzsche (1844–1900), W. B. Yeats (1865–1939), T. S. Eliot (1888–1965), Patrick White (1912–90), and many others—and in all of Indian languages, have admired or drawn upon Sanskrit literature, its style, myths, and metaphors.

What is it about Sanskrit that keeps the universal fascination for it continuing for centuries, even for a millennium after it ceased to be the primary language of literary production in India? And indeed, what is it about Sanskrit which makes it one of the most pre-eminent languages of the world? Historically, the spread and the influence of Latin as well as English increased through their empire-building. In contrast, during the long history of its existence, Sanskrit does not appear to have been consciously promoted by any long-standing empire. Magadhi, a contemporary Prakrit, was of importance to the Mauryan empire.

Emperor Ashoka's inscriptions were in Prakrit, written in Brahmi or Kharoshti scripts, and also in Aramaic or Greek. Sanskrit was used for literary and academic purposes during the Gupta period; but the Prakrits formed the primary medium of communication. The Chalukyas used Kannada or local Prakrits as their primary languages and the Kannada script as their main script. The Satavahana period witnessed the spread and literary growth of several varieties of Prakrit. Persian was the primary language during the Mughal era. Therefore, one cannot equate the power and spell of Sanskrit with that of Latin in ancient Europe or English in recent centuries. Arabic, initially a local speech variety of Mecca, spread over North Africa, Iberia, and China during the seventh-century Islamic conquests. It also spread through the nomadic Arab merchants moving along the medieval trade routes such as the Silk Road. Unlike Arabic and English, the history of Sanskrit does not indicate its spread through either war or commerce. The Chinese empire grew and spread over vast areas through marriage alliances between dynasties and several mergers of their territories. All through its history, propagation of a certain speech variety or script-style took place primarily through conscious decisions by the rulers. While it would be partially incorrect to say that Sanskrit lacked in royal patronage, it would also be incorrect to claim that Sanskrit ever rode on the back of any empire. And yet it impacted quite pervasively the lives and thoughts of people across Asia, and beyond.

Perhaps, determining the origin of Sanskrit and the precise course of its development from the earliest times has been the most absorbing interest for Western scholars as also for those from India over the last two centuries. Enormous intellectual energy has been spent on specifying the exact genealogy of Sanskrit—its exact period of origin, its clear ancestry, and family connections—as well as its anatomy—linguistic features, grammar, and word-stock. It would be an understatement to say that those scholarly efforts have substantially contributed to the world's understanding of Sanskrit. But, despite the vast intellectual enterprise, there still are some unresolved aspects of the emergence, growth, and decline of Sanskrit. These unresolved issues include the precise period of the formation of Sanskrit as a language, and its first use of script. Pitched debates have emerged for more than a century and revolved around questions such as: 'When and where did Sanskrit take birth?'; 'Did it travel from its original birthplace to South Asia, or did it travel from India to other parts of the world?'; 'Was there a script in use in the Indus Valley civilization?'; and 'If what was used was indeed a script, was it or was it not a script associated with Sanskrit, making the emergence of Sanskrit that much older?' These questions can be summed up in popular phrases such as 'the Aryan migration' debate and 'the Indus script' debate.

Though no commentator in our time can discuss Sanskrit without addressing these two pitched debates, I shall not enter those debates for the fear of repeating what has already been said by many eminent subject experts in Human Genetics, Anthropology, and Archaeology. Rather, I would like to raise and answer—at least tentatively—a question that, I believe, has not been raised and addressed so far. That question is 'Why, despite rarely being a "mainstream" language, did Sanskrit come to acquire such an amazingly large clout, such great prestige, and such a long life?' I should add that when I describe it as 'not a mainstream' language, I do not in the least imply that every non-mainstream language is a 'marginal' language. The linguistic history of South Asia does not permit the two terms to be used as direct antonyms. That clichéd binary between the mainstream and the marginal is best left out of the discussion related to a phenomenal linguistic tradition called Sanskrit. Let me offer an illustration.

Just in one single field of scientific enquiry of language, what is generally known as grammar, or 'Vyakarana' as Sanskrit named it, the Sanskrit language produced an impressive and long line of thinkers. The name of Panini (fifth century BCE) has come to be synonymous with grammar. But there have been his predecessors of uncertain dates such as Apishali, Kashyapa, Gargya, Galava, Cakravarmana, Bharadvaja, Shakatayana, Shakalya, Senaka, and Sphotayana. Their works have not survived, but the mention of their work has. Then there was Yaska (seventh century BCE), and Patanjali (author of *Mahabhashya*, second century BCE). Bhartrihari (fifth century CE) is perhaps as widely known and as influential as Panini. In comparison, Jayaditya (seventh century CE), Vamana (seventh century CE), and Helaraja (tenth century CE) are not so well-known. The

Sanskrit 'Vyakarana' tradition continued in the second millennium through Maitreya-rakshita (twelfth and thirteenth centuries CE), Padmanabhadatta (fourteenth century CE), Bhattoji Dikshita (seventeenth century CE), and Kaunda Bhatta (seventeenth century CE). Beyond the seventeenth century, and through the colonial period, the area has continued to attract scholars such as James R. Ballantyne (1838), W. D. Whitney (1879), R. G. Bhandarkar (1888), Friedrich Max Müller (1893), Belvalkar (1915), Arthur MacDonell (1927), Thomas Burrow (1955), and J. H. Stall (1972). Obviously, it makes no sense to describe this impressive tradition of grammarians as a 'minor tradition' in India's intellectual history. That simply cannot be said. What, however, needs to be said is that in almost all cases of these grammarians, the segment of the entire language stock of South India being brought under their respective systems of grammar was relatively small in most of those different times. In that very limited and qualified sense, I use the term 'non-mainstream', not in order to belittle a great tradition, but rather the very opposite, that is, to show why it can be described as a great tradition, while not being the main tradition. My focus is to explain and understand the trajectory of Sanskrit over the last thirty-five centuries and a paradox at its heart, which has not received the scrutiny it deserves. As a part of my argument alludes to the originary moment of the language and also the question of its orthography, I shall briefly sum up the two prevalent debates for clearing some of the popular beliefs about Sanskrit. However, before we turn to those debates and to an overview of how this tradition came to be perceived also as the main tradition, it may help to recount some facts related to the Sanskrit language in our more recent history.

## THE MODERN PERCEPTIONS

One of the most important debates in the Constituent Assembly related to the linguistic future of India took place on 13 September 1949. Dr Rajendra Prasad (1884–1963) chaired the debate. Pandit Lakshmi Kanta Maitra (1895–1953), a member of the assembly elected from Bengal, participated in it to propose that English be used as India's 'official language' for a short initial period, but be replaced by Sanskrit after the initial period was over. The 9th volume of the *Constituent*

*Assembly Debates* carries the verbatim transcript of his argument. He made one more demand: to include Sanskrit in the list of 'scheduled' languages. These two demands he defended through a passionate, though unsubstantiated, plea:

> I have got another substantial amendment, namely the addition of Sanskrit in the list of the languages of the Union. It is surprising that before my amendment was tabled, none even considered the desirability of recognizing Sanskrit as one of the languages of India. That is the depth to which we have fallen. I make absolutely no apology for asking you seriously to accept Sanskrit. Who is there in this country who will deny that Sanskrit is the language of India? I am surprised that an argument was trotted out that it is not an Indian language, that it is an international language. Yes, it is an international or rather a world language in the sense that its importance, its wealth, its position, its grandeur has [*sic*] made it transcend the frontiers of India and travel far beyond India, and it is because of the Sanskrit language and

all the rich heritage of Indian culture that is enshrined in it that outside India we are held in deep esteem by all countries.[1]

One of the members present in the constituent assembly asked Pandit Maitra if he would offer to speak a few sentences in Sanskrit. He brushed aside the embarrassing question, and continued to argue in favour of replacing English with Sanskrit in the near future. The reasons he forwarded were: Sanskrit will keep India united; the world respects India because of the Sanskrit language; if the newly created Israel can foreground Hebrew, why should India not foreground Sanskrit? But mainly, the West expects India to teach it the wisdom that the Sanskrit language developed in the past:

> Sir, Sanskrit has the oldest and the most respectable pedigree of all the languages in the world. I have got here a collection of opinions of some of the biggest orientalists that the world has ever produced; the consensus of opinion of men like Max Müller, Keith, Taylor, Sir William Hunter,

---

[1] *Constituent Assembly Debates*, Volume 9, 13 September 1949, Constitution of India.

Sir William Golebuk, Seleigman, Schopenhauer, Goethe, not to speak of numerous other people like Macdonell and Dubois. All have accorded to Sanskrit the highest place, not to please us, because when these opinions were expressed, we were a subject race under a foreign power.... These great servants unhesitatingly declared that Sanskrit was 'the oldest and the richest language of the world,' 'the one language of the world,' 'the mother of all languages of the world'...I know it will be said that it is a dead language. Yes. Dead to whom?...If Sanskrit is dead, may I say that Sanskrit is ruling us from her grave? Nobody can get away from Sanskrit in India...We should give our message to the West. The West is steeped in materialistic civilisation. The Message of the Gita, the Vedas, the Upanishads and the Tantras, the Charaka and Susrutha etc., will have to be disseminated to the West. It is thus and thus alone that we may be able to command the respect of the world—not by our political debates, nor by our scientific discoveries which, compared with their achievements, are nothing. The West looks to you to give them guidance in this war-torn world where morals are shattered, and religious and spiritual life have gone to shambles.

The amendment was rejected by the Assembly, but Sanskrit found a place in the list of fourteen languages included in the Eighth Schedule of the Constitution. They were Assamese, Bengali, Gujarati, Hindi, Kannada, Kashmiri, Malayalam, Marathi, Odia, Punjabi, Sanskrit, Tamil, Telugu, and Urdu. Of these, thirteen were contemporary and in active use by large numbers of speakers. The one that was not in use as a 'home language' was Sanskrit. It was not as if the language was not understood by anyone, like a dead language that no one comprehends. It was in use for scriptural purposes and in literary transactions. It had continued to provide lexical components for forming new compound words in most other languages placed in the Eighth Schedule. But it no longer was a language in full circulation.

The 1931 Census of India led by J. H. Hutton had not mentioned Sanskrit as a 'spoken language' in any part of British India, while it had mentioned in the 'Subsidiary Table-371' a number of branches of 'Indo-

European Family' such as Assamese, Balochi, Bengali, Bihari, Kachin, Kashmiri, Lahanda, Marathi, Odia, Punjabi, Pashto, Shina, and Sindhi. In the background of Hutton's census was George Abraham Grierson's exhaustive survey of the languages being spoken in India at the beginning of the twentieth century. He reported 179 languages and 544 dialects. While he discusses Sanskrit as a past language, a language which combined with several other 'outer' varieties of that language or other pre-existing languages to produce the languages prevalent in his times, he does not mention Sanskrit as a language in use in India of his time. A decade after the Constitution and its Eighth Schedule were adopted, another census was conducted in 1961. It reported use of 1,652 'mother tongues'. The total number of persons who claimed Sanskrit as their mother tongue in this census was 1,849, whereas the speakers of all other Indo-Aryan languages were 321,720,700; approximately less than one Sanskrit speaker per million Indians. In later census records, the number of Sanskrit speakers varies. A decade later, in 1971, the number was 2,212. It grew in 1981 to 6,106, and in 1991 to 49,736. Perhaps, the growth appears to be some error in computation, for in

2001, the number of speakers had drastically reduced to just 14,135; and in 2011 it was 24,821, just half of the speakers twenty years earlier. In short, the government statistics produced in various decades over the last hundred years clearly indicate that Sanskrit no longer enjoys existence as a spoken language. It continues to exist, but only as a legacy language rather than an active language. That indeed has been its condition all through the last millennium. This situation can be visualized with a greater clarity when one compares the trajectory of Sanskrit in India with that of the Persian language. Persian came into use with the establishment of the first sultanate in 1206 CE. In terms of literary history, it is the era of Amir Khusrau (1253–1325). The sultanates that favoured Persian primarily comprised Hindvi, Arabic, and Turkic speakers. But the Persian language continued to grow. It came into widespread use for official and literary purposes, as a kind of class and culture acquisition, in areas as far-flung as the Deccan, Bengal, Maharashtra, Kashmir, Delhi, and Agra. The majority of people in those areas had their own languages, which too had been rapidly developing precisely through the same time frame all at the same time. Finally, Persian declined with the colonial government deciding to replace it with the regional and native languages such as Marathi, Gujarati, Telugu, Bangla, etc., in 1837. Mirza Ghalib (1797–1869) was, perhaps, the last major poet in that long tradition. In comparison to the millennia-long history of Sanskrit, the half-a-millennium history of Persian is short. Yet, the pattern of spread is not very different, the principle being that a language brought in by a relatively very small number of people acquires a high status and impacts the thought, literature, and life of the entire subcontinent, and an active exchange between it and the local languages effects linguistic transformation of both.

Literary records indicate that at the turn of the first millennium CE, Sanskrit had already started losing its centrality to intellectual and philosophic activity. In the next few centuries, poets and thinkers kept gravitating towards the emerging regional languages. However, that should not take away from Sanskrit the glory of being one of the most remarkable of the languages the world has ever known. If one were to estimate as to how many Indians might have spoken Sanskrit in the past, one can refer to Tim Dyson's *A Population*

*History of India: From the First Modern People to the Present Day.* Dyson estimates that the population of South Asia during the Indus Valley civilization period (twenty-fifth century BCE to nineteenth century BCE) may have been about 4 to 6 million people, growing to 35 million at the beginning of the Common Era, and to 187 million by 1800 CE.[2] These figures are scientifically calibrated estimates; and the map of prehistoric India was significantly different from its present map. Nonetheless, considering that people in the south, east, and north-east had their own languages, and further considering that not the people of all varnas used Sanskrit, one can assign an approximate number of Sanskrit speakers to a few thousand during the early Rig Vedic period (fourteenth century BCE), rising over the next thousand years to about a million—adults and children—during Panini's time, not geographically concentrated but scattered over a vast area stretching from present-day Afghanistan, Pakistan, and Punjab, to the land of Yamuna and Ganga. The population of Sanskrit-knowing people, perhaps, never substantially

---

[2] Tim Dyson, *A Population History of India: From the First Modern People to the Present Day*, Oxford: Oxford University Press, 2018.

exceeded this figure, and continued to decline from the sixth century to the tenth century, bringing it down to negligible numbers. All linguistic, cultural, and political details indicate that through the last thousand years, the number of Sanskrit-knowing Indians kept reducing and remained a minuscule portion of India's ever-growing population. In my opinion, the small numbers of Sanskrit-speaking people is not a negative reflection on it but rather a testimony of its amazing ability to exert influence on the lives and thoughts of those who did not speak or understand Sanskrit.

It is generally assumed that modern India's somewhat disproportionate pride in Sanskrit originates in the unexpected compliments it received from Sir William Jones in his 'Third Anniversary Discourse to the Asiatic Society' delivered on 2 February 1786. It is undeniable that the hypothesis on a prehistoric common origin of Greek, Latin, Sanskrit, and Iranian he put forward in that historic speech inaugurated a glorious chapter in Historical Linguistics and Comparative Etymology. It is also true that Jones's address[3] altogether transformed

---

[3] William Jones, 'The Third Anniversary Discourse (delivered 2 February 1786) by the president at the Asiatic Society of Bengal', ELIOHS.

several fields of scholarly enquiry. Jones was transparent about the historical framework within which he wanted to examine the hypothesis. At one end of it was an open and undefined remote past. At the other end was the eleventh century, the time when Islamic conquerors established a hold over much of Indian territory. The map of that territory extended from the east of Iran all the way to Java in the east. This was much before what later came to be the British Indian empire:

> I begin with *India,* not because I find reason to believe it the true centre of population or of knowledge, but, because it is the country, which we now inhabit, and from which we may best survey the regions around us; as, in popular language, we speak of the *rising* sun, and of his *progress through the Zodiack,* although it had long ago been imagined, and is now demonstrated, that he is himself the centre of our planetary system. Let me here premise, that, in all these inquiries concerning the history of *India,* I shall confine my researches downwards to the *Mohammedan* conquests at the beginning of the *eleventh* century, but extend

them upwards, as high as possible, to the earliest authentic records of the human species.

*India* then, on its most enlarged scale, in which the ancients appear to have understood it, comprises an area of near forty degrees on each side, including a space almost as large as all *Europe;* being divided on the west from *Persia* by the *Arachosian* mountains, limited on the east by the *Chinese* part of the farther peninsula, confined on the north by the wilds of *Tartary,* and extending to the south as far as the isles of *Java.* This trapezium, therefore, comprehends the stupendous hills of *Potyid* or *Tibet,* the beautiful valley of *Cashmir,* and all the domains of the old *Indoscythians,* the countries of *Nepál* and *Butánt, Cámrùp* or *Asàm,* together with *Siam, Ava, Racan,* and the bordering kingdoms, as far as the *Chína* of the *Hindus* or *Sín* of the Arabian Geographers; not to mention the whole western peninsula with the celebrated island of *Sinhala,* or *Lion-like* men, at its southern extremity. By *India,* in short, I mean that whole extent of country, in which the primitive religion and languages of the

*Hindus* prevail at this day with more or less of their ancient purity, and in which the *Nagari* letters are still used with more or less deviation from their original form.

Having started with a puranic version of India, and having cancelled out the history of eight centuries immediately preceding his time, he then moves on to say why Sanskrit travelled into India, from a location and a language stock which also may be the original location and language stock for the classical languages mentioned by him:

> The *Sanscrit* language, whatever be its antiquity, is of a wonderful structure; more perfect than the *Greek*, more copious than the *Latin*, and more exquisitely refined than either, yet bearing to both of them a stronger affinity, both in the roots of verbs and in the forms of grammar, than could possibly have been produced by accident; so strong indeed, that no philologer could examine them all three, without believing them to have sprung from some common source, which, perhaps, no longer exists: there is a similar reason, though not quite

so forcible, for supposing that both the *Gothick* and the *Celtick,* though blended with a very different idiom, had the same origin with the *Sanscrit;* and the old *Persian* might be added to the same family, if this were the place for discussing any question concerning the antiquities of *Persi.*

Jones's hypothesis hit the European world of scholarship like a storm. For the next hundred years, Linguistics turned predominantly historical and comparative and delved deep into the lexical connections between Iranian, Latin, Greek, Sanskrit, Slav, Gothic, and several more languages. By the time Ferdinand de Saussure (1857–1913) brought language scholarship back to Structural Linguistics, the amount of research devoted to proving Jones's hypothesis had brought to life not only the last of these languages but also a powerful myth surrounding the ancient people who were the first speakers of the Proto-Indo-European. Towards the end of the nineteenth century, the myth had a vice-like grip on the minds of French and German linguists. It later turned into the most brutal politics the world had ever seen, the politics of fascism. In India, the myth fit well with the wishful pride of an enslaved India. It was the myth of the proto-historic Aryans.

Before I turn to addressing the Aryan question in relation to the Sanskrit language, let me add that it was not only Sanskrit that drew the scholarly and cultural attention of European scholars. Tamil, too, did so in no less a measure, as is evident from the works on Tamil language, society, and the southern theological schools beginning in the seventeenth century with Portuguese Jesuit, Henrique Henriques (1520–1600); the Italian Jesuit, Roberto de Nobili (1577–1656); and the German Lutheran, Bartholomäus Ziegenbalg (1682–1719). The interest continued through the times of Colin Mackenzie (1754–1821), the first Surveyor General of India and British civil servant in the Madras Presidency; and scholar of Tamil and Sanskrit, F. W. Ellis (1777–1819), who spent years collecting palm-leaf manuscripts in the Tamil area, including the highly significant Tamil works of the Italian Jesuit, Constanzo Beschi (1680–1747). Ellis and British missionary and linguist Robert Caldwell (1814–91) did for Tamil what Sir William Jones did for Sanskrit, namely, placing Tamil as the fountainhead of the Dravidian language family. Their interest went much beyond only the Tamil language, to the Tamil society and its ethical codes. The rise of the Dravidian Movement owes a great deal to George Uglow Pope (1820–1908) who published his monumental translation and study of the *Tiruvacakam*, a volume of Tamil hymns composed by the ninth-century Shaivite Bhakti poet Manikkavasagar.[4] The interest in Tamil continued to attract European scholars such as Czech linguist Kamil Zvelebil (1927–2009), author of *Tamil Literature* (1975); and Israeli Indologist David Schulman (b. 1949) who published a comprehensive cultural history of Tamil language, literature, and civilization entitled *Tamil: A Biography* (2016). Thus, Tamil, too, received attention from European scholars over the last four centuries, increasing its esteem. Yet, the kind of pride that a certain class of Indians takes in Sanskrit far surpasses the respect it has for Tamil. Likewise, Kannada, too, received continued interest from European missionaries, scholars, and colonial administrators such as German scholar Ferdinand Kittel (1832–1903), known for *A Kannada–English Dictionary*

[4] Hudson, Dennis, 'The Responses of Tamils to Their Study by Westerners 1608-1908', *Comparative Civilizations Review*, Vol. 13, No. 13, Article 14, 1985.

(1894); German missionary Hermann Mögling (1811–81) who translated well-known Kannada classics; British historian, archaeologist, and educationist Benjamin Lewis Rice (1837–1927); British historian, epigraphist, and linguist J. F. Fleet (1847–1917) who edited Kannada ballads and folk songs; and Reverend William Reeve (1794–1850), author of an early dictionary of the Kannada language and translator of the Bible into Kannada. John Garrett (1815–93), a polyglot and a Wesleyan missionary, established the first printing press and produced works on Indian languages, and German missionary Friedrich Ziegler produced the *English-Kannada Dictionary* (1868). Marathi, too, attracted the scholarly attention of William Carey (1761–1834), the English missionary who founded the Serampore College and the Serampore University; and prominent lexicographer of the Marathi language, James Thomas Molesworth (1795–1871). One can go on adding names of such scholars engaged in the study of almost all of the Indian languages. Bangla received perhaps the maximum attention beginning with the scholars of the Asiatic Society in the closing years of the eighteenth century. During the early twentieth century, Bangla had received a Nobel Prize in literature (1913), for *Gitanjali* by Rabindranath Tagore (1861–1941). Tagore had won admiration from some of the leading writers of his time: W. B. Yeats (1865–1939), André Gide (1869–1951), and Ezra Pound (1885–1972). And yet, if it was Sanskrit that was seen by most Indians as the language admired by the West, there had to be a reason beyond William Jones's inauguration of Comparative Etymology and Historical Linguistics. Before we move to understanding that reason, let us briefly visit the two debates that have currently brought Sanskrit into the arena of non-linguistic and ideological arguments.

## MISGUIDED DEBATES

As a strange coincidence in history, almost about the same time that Jones hit upon the idea of a common ancestral or 'proto' version of several European languages connected in the remote past with Sanskrit, another chance linguistic discovery emerged from Africa and excited Europe. This was the discovery of the Rosetta Stone carrying Egyptian hieroglyphs, demotic script, and ancient Greek in 1799 by a soldier in Napoleon's army. French philologist Jean-François Champollion deciphered it in 1822. The decipherment took Europe's sense of the past back by nearly twenty-five centuries. The two intellectual developments, one in India, another in Egypt, brought Linguistics and Epigraphy closer, greatly spurring the historical curiosity of researchers. There were many such scripts to decipher: the Meroitic in Sudan, the Etruscan alphabets in Greece, the Aegean Linear A in Crete, the Proto-Elamite in Iran, the Rongorongo of the Easter Island, the Zapotic and Isthmian in Mexico, the Mayan glyphs in Central America, and the Linear B in Greece. By the time English architect, classicist, and philologist Michael Ventris (1922–56), led by his intuition, unravelled Linear B, the science of script decipherment had made great advances. The 1950s saw two more successful decipherments: Babylonian cuneiform by British orientalist Sir Henry Creswicke Rawlinson (1810–95), and the Mayan script by Soviet and Russian linguist, epigraphist, and ethnologist Yuri Knorozov (1922–99). In India, English archaeologist Sir John Marshall's edited book *Mohanjo-Daro and the Indus Civilization* had come out in 1931 (London: Arthur Probsthain); and it had become known to the world that a number of seals were found during the Indus excavation. So, another script was asking for decipherment. The time span of Indus Valley civilization—twenty-fifth century BCE to nineteenth century BCE—heightened the interest of researchers in what has come to be known as the Indus script.

British author of more than thirty books on scripts, decipherment, and the evolution of writing, Andrew Robinson (b. 1957), has traced the history of the attempts to decipher eleven such ancient and mysterious scripts, and records that several score attempts have been made at the decipherment of the Indus script, but none so far has accomplished complete success. He states that 'there can be shibboleth by which we judge a script to be undeciphered or deciphered; we must instead talk about degrees of decipherment. The most useful criterion is the degree to which the proposed decipherment can generate consistent reading from new samples of the script, preferably produced by persons other than the original decipherer'.[5] Judged against this criterion, Robinson finds that out of the numerous attempts made so far, only five or six could achieve a moderate degree of success in deciphering the Indus script. Its conclusively

---

[5] Andrew Robinson, *Lost Languages: The Enigma of the Undeciphered Scripts,* New York: McGraw-Hill, 2002, p. 18.

definitive decipherment is as yet a distant dream. The few attempts which Robinson isolates for analysis are by the celebrated Egyptologist Sir Flinders Petrie (1853–1942), Cambridge-based Assyriologist James Kinnier Wilson (1921–2022), American archaeologist Walter Fairservis (1921–94), and former director of the Archaeological Survey of India, Dr S. R. Rao (1922–2013). Each made some headway, but none has managed to unravel the script fully. One major difficulty in their research is the insufficient number of seals and tablets available for examination, but the most crucial challenge is that we do not know which language the script represents.

In the case of the Egyptian and the Mesopotamian, researchers had other language samples available to match either with the script being deciphered or with the language the script represented. With the Indus script, its obscurity increases as we do not have any clue about the language it represents. Considering that the Indus civilization had spread over a very large area, almost one-fourth of the size of Europe, it may have been not just one language but several languages. But scholars still do not know which one or which ones. Therefore, the outcome of any attempt at decipherment of the script is likely to remain limited to the structural aspects and orthography, and it will never be possible to link the letters to sentences and the communication in the language that it represents. In Robinson's words, 'How far is it possible to advance purely by internal analysis of the inscriptions, without taking a stab at guessing the Indus language?'[6] It is here that the Sanskrit is brought into the scene.

The arrival of Sanskrit (fourteenth century BCE) in India has been dated at almost five centuries after the Indus civilization declined (nineteenth century BCE). Yet, wishful attempts are made to show that what the Indus people spoke was Sanskrit, or one of its earlier forms. Often, one hears spurious claims in social media political propaganda about decipherment of the Indus script and about Sanskrit being the Indus language. All research in Epigraphy, Archaeology, Human Genetics, Anthropology, and Linguistics unambiguously indicates that the claim is untenable. To give credence to it would be as fanciful as claiming that Persian (arrival in the thirteenth century) was spoken in India during

---

[6] Ibid., p. 279.

Kalidasa's times (fourth and fifth centuries), or English was being spoken during the era of the sultanates. As and when in the future we come to know if the seals found in Indus sites are inscribed with characters or signs of a script and, if that is the case, the Indus script gets deciphered, it will be a great addition to the world's knowledge about prehistoric Asia. At present, all that we know is that we do not know enough about the Indus script; we also know that the language it represented was not an older version of Sanskrit. What we also know is that if the Indus seals point to the existence of a script, that script did not survive the Indus period. In human history, there are very rare examples of societies which give up on writing once they have developed the technique of writing. It has to be considered a great mystery why the generations who survived the end of the Indus civilization would have altogether forgotten the art of writing—if writing it at all was—after using it for nearly half a millennium (twenty-fourth century BCE to nineteenth century BCE). There is no known evidence of the presence of any script in the proto-historic and ancient India for the nearly sixteen-centuries-long time span between the decline of the Indus civilization (nineteenth century BCE) and the first inscription in 260 BCE by Emperor Ashoka (third century BCE). Finally, what we know with great certainty is that the language which came to be subsequently recognized as Sanskrit was in existence for a little over a millennium during this long historical span (fourteenth century BCE to third century BCE). The historical fact as we know it beyond doubt is that the use of script emerged through granting rock inscriptions or issuing rock edicts. Ashoka pioneered the practice. The scripts he used ranged from the Brahmi to Kharoshthi and Greek to Aramaic, and the languages in which they were inscribed had Sanskrit in them only in a minor proportion. Andrew Ollett, a significant scholar of ancient Indian languages, comments:

> Ashoka's use of a Middle Indic language, written in the Brahmi script, was extremely influential. Almost all inscriptions in the subcontinent followed this model, apart from Tamil Nadu (which used Brahmi, and later Vatteluttu, to write Tamil) and Gandhara (which used Kharosthi to write a language, now called Gandhari, that began

to rapidly diverge from other forms of Middle India in the first and second century BCE)... Sanskrit inscriptions are in fact extremely rare until the third and especially fourth century BCE, despite the fact that Sanskrit is 'older' in linguistic terms than the Middle Indic languages, and always had a long history of cultivation as a learned language. Louis Renou called this 'the great linguistic paradox of India': not just that Sanskrit was not commonly used for inscriptions before the fourth century or so, but that there was a pronounced shift from the Middle Indic languages towards Sanskrit.[7]

We shall speak about this 'great paradox', its genesis and cultural features in the next chapter, after setting aside another debate related to the Sanskrit language, its origin.

Initiated by William Jones's linguistic hypothesis, over the last two centuries, a number of books have

---

[7] Andrew Ollett, 'Early Inscriptions', in G. N. Devy, Tony Joseph, Ravi Korisettar (eds.), *The Indians: Histories of a Civilization*, New Delhi: Aleph Book Company, 2023, pp. 220–21.

appeared on the Aryan question: who they were, how they migrated, in which direction or directions and when. Several other disciplines such as Archaeology, Anthropology, Cosmology, Mythology, Folklore, Scriptural Studies, Cultural Geography, Biology, Botany, and Genetics have participated in the debate. It finally appears to have arrived at a scientific closure with Human Genetics combined with Linguistics establishing the extent, direction, and the patterns of the migration. The debate is a lot more than a purely linguistic debate. It is much beyond the scope of history owing to the large time spans and the nature of evidence available which Archaeology can handle more effectively than History can. I shall, therefore, place here, three views based on scientific examination to illustrate how science has brought a definitive closure to the debate. In a paper published in the *Iranian Journal of Archaeological Studies* in 2011, anthropologist S. R. Walimbe dismisses the assumed scale of the invasion by people speaking the Indo-Aryan, who are supposed to have destroyed the Indus population and built a new civilization in India. His conclusion is that the mixing of the populations is a post-Indus migration phenomenon and that the mixing was a gradual process and happened in nominal numbers.

It would be interesting to note that, human population genetics data corroborates same physical anthropological inferences, concluding that there is no material evidence for any large-scale migrations into India over the period of 4500 to 800 BCE. Basu *et al.* (2003) examine genetic variation in 44 geographically, linguistically, and socially disparate ethnic populations of India and use U2 frequencies to infer the existence of 'Aryan' movements. U2 comprises two sub-lineages, U2e (European-specific sub-lineage) and U2i (Indian-specific sub-lineage). Basu *et al.* (2003) have shown that U2e is not present in the Indian tribal groups, but only among castes. The U2e frequency is therefore more important in estimating the number of Aryan-speaking people entering India. Such evidence showed a much smaller estimate of migrants, though the actual number is difficult to estimate. Aryan speakers possibly came into

India in small bands over a long period of time, as opposed to in a single wave of migration.[8]

The Aryan migration debate has been active in the past, but ever since Human Genetics started bringing in new evidence about ancient migrations, it has got sharply divided between rational analysis and a tendentious imagination of the past. The division is not just clear; it has got shrill as well. The political ideology of Hindutva is keen on cleaning the Indian society of all 'outside' influences;[9] and it is difficult for it to accept that languages, cultures, and communities have migrated over the surface of the earth in the entire history of the *Homo sapiens*. The inward flow of a language, particularly the one that is the language of many of India's sacred texts, is an idea unpalatable for that political ideology. It is, therefore, ready to use myth or invent evidence to prove the contrary. Objective scientific enquiry does not seem to favour its wish lists. In the February 2025 issue of

---

[8] S. R. Walimbe, 'Aryan Invasion in the Indian Subcontinent: Facts and Fallacies, The Physical Anthropological Perspectives', *Iranian Journal of Archaeological Studies*, Vol. 1, No. 1, 2011, pp. 35–43.
[9] Vinayak Damodar Savarkar, 'Some of the Basic Principles and Tenets of the Hindu Movement', *Hindu Rashtra Darshan*, Bombay: Savarkar Prakashan, 1984, pp. 76–83.

*Nature*, a large international team of scientists led by Iosif Lazaridis of Harvard University has published a paper entitled 'The Genetic Origin of the Indo-Europeans'. Based on ancient DNA of 435 individuals, it draws the conclusion that the mixing of populations in the Yamnaya around the thirty-third century BCE was tripartite and reached its maximum spread by early third millennium BCE. 'The CLV (Caucasus–Lower Volga) people contributed around four-fifths of the ancestry of the Yamnaya and, entering Anatolia, probably from the east, at least one-tenth of the ancestry of Bronze Age central Anatolians, who spoke Hittite. We therefore propose that the final unity of the speakers of 'Proto-Indo-Anatolian', the language ancestral to both Anatolian and Indo-European people, occurred in CLV people sometime between 4400 BCE and 4000 BCE.' The trajectory of the language moving from Yamnaya to the north-western areas of ancient India is worked out in great detail by David W. Anthony in his book, *The Horse, the Wheel, and Language*. He points out that it is unlikely that the initial spread of the Proto-Indo-European dialects into the regions outside Pontic–Caspian steppes was caused by 'an organized invasion' or a 'series of military conquests'.

He compares the movement to a 'franchising operation': 'At last a few steppe chiefs must have moved into each new region, and their initial arrival might well have been accompanied by cattle raiding and violence.'[10] Probably the most important factor in the migration—not massive but small yet speedy groups—was the technologies of horse-rearing and wheeled chariot-like cars. Anthony traces the spread of the Proto-Indo-European from some fifty-second century BCE, first to Yamnaya and, from there to other parts of Asia and Europe. He notices two major social institutions along this trajectory: 'The first institution, legalizing inequality, probably was very old, going back to the initial acceptance of the herding economy, about 5200–5000 BCE, and the first appearance of pronounced differences in wealth. The second might have developed to regulate migration into unregulated geographic and social space at the beginning of the Yamnaya horizon.'[11] He adds, 'The Yamnaya horizon exploded across the Pontic Caspian steppes about 3300 BCE. With it probably went Proto-Indo-European, its

---

[10] David W. Anthony, *The Horse, the Wheel, and Language*, Princeton: Princeton University Press, 2007, p. 464.
[11] Ibid., p. 461.

dialects scattering as its speakers moved apart, their migrations sowing the seeds of Germanic, Baltic, Slavik, Italic, Celtic, Armenian and Phrygian.'[12]

> The heroic world of chariot-driving warriors was dimly remembered in the poetry of the *Iliad* and the *Rig Veda*. It was introduced to the civilizations of Central Asia and Iran about 2100 BCE.... Between 2000 and 1800 BCE first Petrovka and then Alakul-Andronovo groups settled in the Zeravshan valley and began mining copper and tin.... The Old Indic religion probably emerged among northern-derived immigrants in the contact zone between the Zeravshan and Iran as a syncretic mixture of old Central Asian and new Indo-European elements. From this time forward the people of the Eurasian steppes remained directly connected with the civilizations of Central Asia, south Asia and Iran, and through intermediaries, with China.[13]

The Vedic period of history, beginning in the fourteenth century BCE, is inaugurated by the Rig Veda and brought

---

[12] Ibid., p. 462.
[13] Ibid.

to culmination by Yaska in the sixth century BCE. The small bands of the Indo-Aryan-speaking people who arrived in the northwest, present-day Afghanistan and Pakistan, slowly spread through Punjab to the Yamuna–Ganga area during that long and culturally phenomenal millennium. In the process, the early Indo-Aryan speech had changed, through elaborate interaction with the pre-existing languages in the area, creating what is known as Sanskrit to us. The debates about its origin cannot be kept confined to the ideas of modern nations, territories, and identities of people. Imposing such ideas amounts to anachronism. Laura Spinney's landmark account of the prehistory of all Indo-European languages establishes how the several-millennia-long trajectory of the Indic branch of the Indo-Iranian languages spans most parts of Eurasia, West Asia, and South Asia. It takes back the prehistory of Sanskrit to the Ural Mountains, Persepolis, Syria, and present-day Afghanistan. Spinney's work demonstrates with great clarity how it would be wrong to look at the history of language by restricting it within the framework of nations or ethnicity. The languages such as Sanskrit, Persian, Greek, and Latin, having a life spread over several millennia, clearly defy those frameworks.[14]

At the time Panini developed his system of grammar in the fifth century BCE, Sanskrit had chosen to remain without a script. As Panini's grammar clearly shows, it was in no way the only language in India, including in the parts where Sanskrit had spread. The post-Panini Sanskrit produced an extraordinarily illuminating corpus of poetry, drama, and philosophy. So did some other languages such as Tamil, Pali, and Prakrit. However, the Vedic language had invented a cultural construct of extraordinary power which other Indian languages of the time never imagined creating. Perhaps, there is no parallel in any language in the world to the inventiveness which Sanskrit displayed in evolving the cultural construct. Therefore, setting aside the misleading controversies surrounding the origin of Sanskrit, I shall turn to discussing its unique creation.

---

[14] Laura Spinney, *Proto: How One Ancient Language Went Global*, London: William Collins, 2025.

II

# THE MEMORY MAGIC AND LANGUAGE HEGEMONY

The unique creation of Sanskrit was an unparalleled oral tradition far surpassing instead of creating any orthographic system. More or less the same time when the Indo-Aryan language started evolving its first branch in South Asia were emerging the ancient Greek (1450 BCE), ancient Chinese (1250 BCE), Aramaic (1100 BCE), and Hebrew (1000 BCE). Some other languages, beginning with the Egyptian, had already developed their scripts. These include: the Sumerian, Hattic, and Elamite language isolates, Hurrian from the small Hurro–Urartian family, Afro–Asiatic in the form of the Egyptian and Semitic languages, and Indo-European such as Anatolian languages and

Mycenaean Greek. Besides, there are some scripts such as the Proto-Elamite script, the Indus script, Cretan hieroglyphs, Linear A, and the Cypro–Minoan syllabary, awaiting to be deciphered. Of course, writing cannot be considered the only proof of the existence of an ancient language. For example, the oldest Avestan texts—the Gathas—are believed to have been composed before 1000 BCE, but the oldest Avestan manuscripts date from the thirteenth century BCE. The Vedic Indo-Aryan language created literary records in the form of the Vedas, but for generations it continued to be transmitted entirely orally. Not all oral traditions in human history are mere assemblages of chance stories and songs. Not all oral societies can be dismissed as 'primitive'. The pastoral bands which became the bridge between the Indo-European and India were certainly not primitive. They had already evolved well-organized social conventions, particularly the contract system between the host and the guest (the yajaman system), well-set methods of alliances (marriage within one's 'kula' and 'gotra'), and ritual offerings to divinities. Besides, they had developed remarkable traditions of poetry and myth—which subsequently surface in the epics in Greece and India. David W. Anthony observes, 'Their social system was maintained by myths, rituals, and institutions that were adopted by others, along with the poetic language that conveyed their prayers to the gods and ancestors. Long after the genetic imprint of the original immigrant chiefs faded away, the system of alliances, obligations, myths and rituals that they introduced was still being passed on from generation to generation.'[15] The oral poetic creation of the earliest of the Vedic singers, therefore, was not made of a chance and sentimental outburst. It was already rooted in a tradition of myth, cosmology, and a world view. The Rig Veda gave the cosmology, myth, and ritual an unparalleled mechanics of memory. English Indologist Ralph T. H. Griffith in his preface to *The Hymns of the Rigveda* observes:

> Rhyme is not used in the Rigveda. The meters are regulated by the number of syllables in the stanza, which consists generally of three or four Padas, measures, divisions, or quarter verses, with a distinctly marked interval at the end of the second Pada, and so forming two *hemistiches* or

---

[15] Anthony, *The Horse, The Wheel, and Language*, p. 464.

semi-stanzas of equal or unequal length. These Padas most usually contain eight or eleven or twelve syllables each; but occasionally they consist of fewer and sometimes of more than these numbers. The Padas of a stanza are generally of equal length and of more or less corresponding prosodic quantities: but at times two or more kinds of meters are employed in one stanza, and then the Padas vary in quantity and length. As regards quantity, the first Syllables of the Pada are not subject to very strict laws, but the last four are more regular, their measure being generally iambic in Padas of eight and twelve syllables and trochaic in those of eleven.

The verses are organized, in ascending order, in terms of 'rik' (verse praising a deity), 'sukta' (a small group of mantras or verses), 'anuvak' (a complete section containing several suktas or sub-sections), and 'mandala' (a 'book' as in an epic or a set of suktas). There are ten mandalas, eighty-five anuvaks, and 1,028 suktas in the Rig Veda (or Rik-veda), constituting a total of 10,552 'mantras'. Scholars tend to think that it may have taken a century or a little longer to develop this vast body of Vedic verses. Since then, for the last thirty-three centuries, the entire corpus gets recited in Ved-pathshalas (where a disciplined recitation of Vedas is taught from generation to generation) by committing it to memory, literally syllable by syllable, almost entirely in the same way as its original composers—the makers of these richas or the rishis—may have recited them three millennia ago. The architecture of the verses—their meters, syllabic arrangement, caesuras, rhythm—was moulded to make their memorization possible for any well-trained reciter of the corpus. The amazing mnemonics has hardly a parallel. The ingenuity of its method perhaps can be compared with the method which the German polymath Gottfried Leibniz (1646–1716) invented, in another continent and in another time, for bringing taxonomies used in diverse disciplines under the rubric of a single 'universal knowledge'. However, I would like to add that the analogy is not intended to support any absurd claim about the Rig Veda having anticipated modern computers resulting out of Leibniz's method; it is purely to underscore the remarkable insight which the composers of the Veda had into the nature of human memory. A profound understanding of the interlocking of the poetic meter and the working of memory was the principal feature of the Vedic mnemonics.

In order to grasp the genius of the Vedic poets, it may help to mention that English poetry works mainly within five meters: iambic, trochaic, and spondaic having two-syllable feet; and anapaestic and dactylic having three-syllable feet. Compare these with the amazing range of the Vedic meters such as, principally, the Gayatri, Ushnih, Anushtubh, Brihati, Pankti, Trishtubh, Jagati, and additionally, the Atijagati, Shakkari, Atishakkari, Ashti, Atyashti, Dhriti, Atidhriti, Kriti, Prakriti, Akriti, Vikriti, Sanskriti, Atikriti, and Utkriti.

The intricate metrical system could aid memorization of the enormous corpus of the Rig Veda, just as the multiplication table helps in solving difficult sums in a fraction of a second. Besides, in each mandala of the Rig Veda, the hymns are placed in a descending order of the number of stanzas in it; and if any two hymns have equal number of stanzas, then the number of syllables determine their sequence. Thus, the organizational principle is 'the more is the higher, the less is the lower'. However, this was not the only method by which the

Rig Veda made itself unparalleled. There was another, much less visible on the surface but uniquely inventive, and it was its symbolism.[16]

Sri Aurobindo (1872–1950), whose approach to the Vedic poetry differs significantly from the approach of the scholars of Sanskrit, comments in a series of essays (1914–17), posthumously published in book form as *The Secret of the Veda* (1956) elucidates this less discussed side of the Vedic language. His view is that the emergence of the early Vedic poetry and fixing of the Vedic chant by Yaska in two versions—one with sandhis, the sound variations caused at the junction of two terms, and the other with the sandhis dissolved—had a considerable time gap of some eight centuries between them. Therefore, the etymologies compiled by Yaska focused on merely the literal sense of the Veda, often making it look like a collection of unrelated prayers, descriptions of wars, and occasions of various yajna rituals. Yaska had made two texts, one aimed at a literal analysis and the other

---

[16] Ralph T. H. Griffith and Arthur Berriedale Keith (trans.), *The Vedas: The Samhitās of the Rig, Yajur (White and Black), Sama, and Atharva*, Jon William Fergus (ed.), CreateSpace Independent Publishing Platform, 2017.

in view of an exact oral reproduction of the original.

Responding to Yaska's handling of the oral Veda tradition, Aurobindo wryly comments, 'Orality illuminates by obscuring.' It is not that he had any doubts about the Vedic recitations being close in their phonetic production to the very original. His argument is that the richas were consciously designed as mystic symbols, not so much as lexical forms. Aurobindo argues that the richas cannot be understood at all except when seen as a compact of psychological symbols, referring primarily to the inner state of mind rather than any outer objects and events at all. He feels that even the Brahmanas, derived from the Vedas centuries later, do not possess the originality of symbols of the Rig Veda. As against the Brahmanas, the Upanishads turned to their primary symbolism, through meditation and not through etymology, and managed to articulate afresh some of the original symbolic meaning, though, in the process, they lost a lot of the semantic richness of the original Vedic text. As a result of these two distinct derivations of the Vedas, Aurobindo argues, the entire education of the Vedas in subsequent centuries lost the ingenuity of the Vedas in merging the textual with the symbolic. 'What they found, they expressed in other terms more intelligible to the age in which they lived.... They were seekers of a higher than verbal truth and used words merely as suggestions for the illumination towards which they were striving.' He adds, 'They knew not or they neglected the etymological sense and employed often a method of symbolic interpretation of component sounds in which it is very difficult to follow them. For this reason, while the Upanishads are invaluable for the light they shed on the principal ideas and on the psychological system of the ancient Rishis, they help us as little as the *Brahmanas* in determining the accurate sense of the texts which they quote.' He concludes that 'their real work was to found *Vedanta* rather than to interpret *Veda*'.[17]

The distinction between the Vedas in the sense of the original and pure, and the Vedanta in the sense of the derived, somewhat obscured and, therefore, constantly referring to the original, has always remained crucial in India's understanding of Sanskrit in all subsequent periods. It is described slightly differently by the use

---

[17] Sri Aurobindo, *The Secrets of the Veda*, Pondicherry: Sri Aurobindo Ashram, 1956/2012, pp. 14–25.

of the terms shruti and smriti, where shruti refers to the Vedas, the principal Upanishads, and some of the immediate Vedang successors, and smriti to the epics, Dharmasutras, Dharmashastras, numerous Bhashyas, and the Nibandhas. Smriti literally means memory, but the orally transmitted Vedas are given the status of shruti, the divine words envisioned by the Vedic rishis. The status 'Shruti' was given to the Vedas, under the belief that they are so perfect and so entirely free of any linguistic blemish that they would be beyond any mortal being to compose them. In that sense they have no 'originator', they are apaurusheya (not composed by any mortal composer).

The belief was—and it continues so—that the Vedas are without a known origin or beginning, and without a possible end, future termination—'anaadi' and 'anant'.

Therefore, the rishis came to be seen as 'the seers', those who envisioned the verses (which have timeless existence and, therefore already existent).

Hence, though the names of the rishis, the patriarchs of the 'families' or the 'schools' to which the mandalas are ascribed, the Rig Veda came to be perceived during the first millennium BCE as 'apaurusheya', 'without an author' or 'authored by no one like an ordinary person'.

The result was that when Kapila (sixth century BCE) laid the foundations of Samkhya, one of the first schools of ancient Indian philosophy, he proposed that since the Vedas are the divinely inspired and 'authorless' words, the ultimate logical validation of a given premise can be found in them alone. In tune with this position, even analytical philosophy in Sanskrit started getting described as 'darshan' (that which is envisioned) rather than as 'thought' (that which is reasoned). During the first millennium, following Kapila, the Sanskrit language produced six schools of philosophy, all called Darshanas, each with engaged debates and detailed arguments, but none really questioning the authority of the Vedas. That was done by Buddhism and the Lokayata of Charvaka in the sixth century BCE. However, the languages used by them differed from Sanskrit. And, in the long cultural tussle between those languages, the languages other than Sanskrit could not get their deserved centrality in India's philosophical tradition. Within the Sanskrit language tradition of thought, if and when Kapila's philosophical framework was challenged at all, the touchstone for logical validity was shifted from the Vedas to language itself, in turn taking it back to the linguistic ingenuity of the Vedas.

Some twenty-five centuries after the Rig Veda was composed, Kashmiri court poet and literary critic Anandavardhana in his *Dhvanyaloka* (ninth century) and the literary theorist Kuntaka in his *Vakrokti Jivita* (tenth century) proposed fascinating semantic theory about the organic relationship between the symbolic and the literal. However, by then, the hiatus between the Vedas and Vedanta had seeped deep in the Indian mind like its irrevocable and primordial memory. Besides, the live tradition of a flawless verbatim recital of the Vedic hymns, coexisting with the shastras and other interpretations, deepened the sense that the Vedas were beyond the grasp except of the ancient rishis, and all that followed were but pale shadows of the original. Such a feeling had already set in even before scripts became stabilized in ancient India. The result was an enormous heightening of the status of the Vedas, some of it justified but much more of it accepted on authority of the conventions of scholarship. A similar status could never be gained by any other scripture, any other philosophy, or any other form or period of poetry in India ever again. By the time of Panini, when the older Indo-Aryan language acquired the form of what we call Sanskrit, the language had already achieved an inviolable status absolutely hinged on the great linguistic and mnemonic accomplishment of the Vedic poetry. Sanskrit may not have much spread in ancient India, but it had something which no other language in Indian history has had in the same measure, the status as 'dev-bhasha', the language of the immortals.

The historiographical attitude towards the mantra literature—the Vedic hymns, the Brahmanas, the Upanishads, and in extreme cases, some Vedangas—corresponded to the cognitive possibility offered by the grammatical category of paroksha past tense. Once Panini, Katyayana, and Patanjali had constructed the enormous vyakarana—machinery to prohibit 'vulgarization' of the bhasha—the Vedic verses began to be treated as if they were divinely and not humanly composed. Vedic literature forms an excellent instance of linguistic creativity fully integrated with the life of the immediate community surrounding it; it is an eloquent commentary on the history of the people who wrote it. Yet scholars in the post-Panini period were encouraged to believe that the

Vedas were gospel, literally heard by the rishis from a divine source. The Vedas became shruti, the Upanishads, smriti. And both were removed from the historical sphere altogether.

During the nineteenth century, many European scholars took an interest in ancient Indian literature. Some of them determined 1500 BCE as the possible date for the earliest of the Vedic compositions. On the other hand, Indian scholars, more particularly Indian philosopher and nationalist Bal Gangadhar Tilak and his followers, argued that the Vedas were composed much earlier—around 4500 BCE.[18] The history of transmission of this literature through a period of the last 3,500 years shows that unparalleled scholarly care and editorial precision have been lavished on it by the generations involved in the process of its transmission. Max Müller has observed that, unlike the Homeric epics, the Vedas make no reference to the art of writing. But no written text, reproduced by different scholiasts and reprinted in different lexical styles, would have succeeded in preserving the original poetic speech in the exact original

---

[18] C. V. Vaidya, *A Literary History of India, Vol.1-Sruti (Vedic) Period*, Pune: Aryabhushan Press, 1930, p. 124.

form to the last and the finest phonetic detail.

That this training formed an essential part of school education in ancient India is evident from the fact that specialist textbooks, companion volumes, and classified indexes were prepared to assist this training. Katyayana (third century BCE), for instance, had prepared a Vedic sarvanukramani—a general index giving the names of the rishis credited with having contributed to the Rig Veda, the exact number of verses associated with each, the chapter and section divisions of the verses, the meters and also the names of gods in whose praise the verses were composed. In terms of historical scholarship in literature, such anukramanis—and there were many—are invaluable. However, the aim of these scholarly exercises was not to enable other scholars to place the shrutis in a historical context and to see them critically. The aim was the exact opposite; it was to abstract the shrutis from the flow of time altogether so that they became timeless and ahistorical. What happened to the Vedas, happened also to the Upanishads as well as the associated Vedic texts. And, though Indians made impressive progress in certain sciences, agriculture, philosophy, and linguistics continuously for a thousand years after the Vedas were composed, the ancient literary scholarship persisted in its belief that the Vedas held literally all knowledge in them, and that no knowledge could surpass that contained in the Vedas. Traces of this historical fallacy survive in India even today. The logical result of making Vedic literature the ultimate authority in the sphere of knowledge was the emergence of a pervasive rhetoric of knowledge which made *authority* a fundamental source of knowledge.

The profound impact of this faith in authority as knowledge on historiography can be seen in works like Kshemaraja's *Pratyabhijnahrdayam*.[19] An eleventh-century Kashmir philosopher and a disciple of Abhinavagupta, Kshemaraja draws an imaginary topography of spiritual fulfilment by describing the descent of the divine into the human world, which, in his opinion, is necessarily followed by a corresponding human ascent. This doctrine of 'recognition' postulates perception as recollection of what was always known: the greater the capacity to 'remember', the higher the human consciousness can ascend in the realm of the

---

[19] Jaideva Singh, *The Doctrine of Recognition: A Translation of Pratyabhijñāhrdayam*, New York: State University of New York Press, 1990.

spirit. His argument that all new knowledge has always been present in the human consciousness, even if momentarily clouded, derived support from the notion of authority vested with sovereignty in the Vedas. And, hence, even if the Vedic texts are supremely historical as documents, and even if the very history of these texts is eloquently inscribed in them, these texts were removed from the sphere of history by a jealously guarded tradition of scholarship. One outcome of the amazing mnemonic structures was the Vedic oral tradition. The other was a non-Vedic oral tradition. However, the task of keeping that alive was handed over to the non-purohit or non-priestly class, for which a convenient term is the 'suta' class.

The distinction between suta literature and mantra literature was proposed by Marathi sociologist and historian S. V. Ketkar, and was approvingly accepted by scholars like Irawati Karve and V. S. Sukhtankar.[20] According to Ketkar, suta (or sauta) literature is 'literature belonging to the sutas, preserved and sung by the sutas and perhaps largely composed by the sutas. This literature

---

[20] Irawati Karve, *Yuganta: The End of an Epoch*, New Delhi: Sangam Books, 1974, pp. 2–3.

embodied the secular political tradition of Sanskrit literature....'[21] According to Karve, a class of people called sutas representing the illegitimate progeny of the kshatriyas, performed various functions at the court.

> They were counsellors and friends of kings, charioteers, and also bards. Some of these moved from place to place, wherever they knew that people were likely to assemble, and told their stories which consisted mainly of exploits of love and adventure of ancient and ruling kings and princes. A book in many respects like the *Mahabharata* was the *Ramayana*, a narrative sung from place to place. Out of these grew a later type of literature called the *Puranas*....[22]

The suta literature was largely an oral and largely non-lexical tradition. In the process of oral transmission the text was changed, enlarged, and to it was also added the history of recitations. Since the suta texts were treated as essential parts of collective memory and collective inheritance, the particulars about their specific historical

---

[21] Ibid.
[22] Karve, *Yuganta*, p. 2.

moments of origin and individual authorships were not considered important in the suta literary canon. The Mahabharata, which is easily the most complex of the suta literary works, offers us glimpses into the history of its making and transmission. Vyasa, to whom the initial authorship of the poem is ascribed and who was an eyewitness to the war described in it, composed it, perhaps under the title Jaya or Itihasa. At that stage, it is believed to have been much shorter in length. The original had perhaps not more than 24,000 verses. Vyasa seems to have taught the epic to five of his pupils who made their own recessions. One of the pupils was Vaishampayana. He recited the epic on the occasion of the serpent-sacrifice ritual performed by King Janamejaya. The great-grandson of Arjuna, and the grandson of Abhimanyu, as depicted in the Mahabharata, Lomharshana, who was present on this occasion, heard it, and recited it again in the hermitage of the sage Shaunaka in the Naimisha forest. By this time, probably, the 24,000 verses of Jaya had already turned into the 60,000 verses of the Mahabharata.[23] But even after this,

---

[23] C. R. Deshpande, *Transmission of the Mahābhārata Tradition: Vyāsa and Vyāsīds*, Shimla: Indian Institute of Advanced Studies, 1978, pp. 7–14.

generations of poets kept adding verses to it. The result is the present version comprising 100,000 verses.

The Ramayana is another important suta text; and the Puranas too are suta texts. Not only scholars, but even common people knew that the Mahabharata was composed first, the Ramayana later, and the Puranas the last; but the cultural centrality of these texts was such that they were or are rarely thought of as merely linguistic compositions. As a result, they were never allowed to belong to the past, or to have an existence that was detached from the collective consciousness. Hence, their historical status as texts was of marginal interest to scholars involved in their transmission. In India, people are rarely self-conscious about the intimate intertextuality of the suta texts and life as it is lived. This phenomenon strikes an outsider as uniquely Indian. American anthropologist Milton Singer, for instance, comments:

> Before I went to India, I knew these stories as occurring in printed books called the *Ramayana*, the *Mahabharata* and the *Bhagvatapurana*, parts of which I had read in translation. This knowledge

gave me a welcome sense of recognition when I heard some of the stories, but it did not prepare me for the rich variety of ways in which they are told and retold. Seldom did I come across an Indian who had read these stories as I did, simply in a book. This is not how they learn them and it is not how they think of them. There is a sense of intimate familiarity with the characters and incidents in references made to Harishchandra, Rama and Sita, Krishna, Arjuna, and Prahlada as if the world of the stories were also the everyday world...The cultural and physical landscapes are literally and imaginatively printed with them.[24]

Thus, the Indian attitude to the suta texts involves the sense of 'the presence of the past' but not of 'the pastness of the past'. The principal subject of suta literature was history itself. Even the Puranas, which have a greatly rambling style of narration, were, in a loose sense,

---

[24] Milton Singer, *When a Great Tradition Modernizes: An Anthropological Approach to Indian Civilization*, New York: Praeger Publishers, 1972, p. 76, quoted in Ludo Rocher, *The Purāṇas: A History of Indian Literature*, Vol. 2, Fasc. 3, Jan Gonda (ed.), Wiesbaden: Otto Harrassowitz, 1986, p. 72.

'historical' records providing information about dynasties and genealogies, and also contain within themselves some historical information about their composition and transmission; but to think of them as 'books' will not be appropriate to their purpose and history. Traditionally, however, suta texts were seen as constituting the continuous collective memory and were not considered as literary events. That is why Naimisharanya, the location of every recitation of the Mahabharata and the Puranas, became an essential part of people's unconscious personality, and Vyasa, the 'author' of these texts, came to be considered a Chiranjiva, an ever-living mortal.

## THE LANGUAGE OF ESTEEM

The varna system was a peculiar, and despicable, creation of the world view originating in the Vedic ethos. The purohit, quite like the Egyptian pharaoh, came to be considered the necessary intermediary between the humans and the divine. The purohit had to know the Vedic chants. Thus, the small class of those who were trained to internalize the complicated mnemonics forming the architecture of the Veda corpus, gained esteem in the society far disproportionate to their material wealth or political clout. The esteem gained by their knowledge of the Sanskrit language turned them into a distinct class of the society, the 'highest class' at that. There does not appear to be any other material or historical reason for the purohits to emerge as the highest varna than the fact of their command over the Sanskrit language. Their patrons, the ones who could protect their ritual practices, got accepted by them as the next varna as the kshatriyas. These had some access to Sanskrit, but no mastery over it. The others who worked in many professions were ranged as the next in the varna hierarchy, as vaishyas. All others, speakers of many local languages and involved in occupations that had nothing much to do with the ritual practices of the purohits, were relegated to the hugely amorphous varna category as the shudras. Since the magic of the original Vedic mnemonics continued its sway through the history of India, the varna-based social segmentation continued to exist and become increasingly coercive. Sanskrit was essentially spoken by a relatively small section of Indian society; but its hegemony pervaded every area of life, culture, and thought, at least until the Bhakti movement started challenging it in the second millennium.

All through the long history of the Sanskrit language, the poets and writers who used it continued to bask in the afterglow of the miraculous mnemonics of the Vedas. The hegemony of Sanskrit led society to turn most of the iconic writers in this long tradition ahistorical. Perhaps, it is therefore that determining the exact dates or historical periods of authors in Sanskrit poses a serious challenge:

> Writing the history of Sanskrit kavya literature along modern historicist and chronological principles has been even more problematic than piecing together the succession of dynastic history in early India. Scholars have long complained of the sparse biographical and 'historical' information that the Sanskrit literary tradition has supplied for its own authors, making the establishment of both absolute and relative chronologies among works and authors an enduring problem for the field. In some literary works and inscriptions, we occasionally come across mention of a poet's father and grandfather, and literary patrons are

sometimes mentioned, but in most cases the information provided is all too brief. The number of texts whose authors can be placed in particular historical contexts remain, as numerous scholars have noted, strikingly limited.[25]

The fact that the canonical status of texts did not depend on the genre in which they were composed but rather on the function they were expected to perform in the sphere of their reception needs to be stressed when we consider the history of Sanskrit literature. Both the shastras and the akshara texts were composed in verse, prose, or a combination of the two. Both were seen as products of known human authorship. And, as against the suta literature and the mantra literature which were turned timeless, the shastras and the akshara literature were freely subjected to the vagaries of literary tastes, shifts in critical views, and the climate of philosophical opinion. Philosophical debate and literary disagreement were the common features of

[25] Daud Ali, 'Verses at the Court of the King: Shifts in the Historical Imagination of the Sanskrit Literary Tradition during the Second Millennium', *Journal of the Royal Asiatic Society*, Series 3, No. 3, January 2022, pp. 13–31.

the scholarly community that developed these two branches of Sanskrit literature. Linguistics and poetics were considered shastras. Between the fourth century BCE and the seventeenth century CE—a period of about 2,000 years—possibly every linguist in India knew about all linguistics scholarship preceding him. He knew the major sutras or theoretical formulations as well as the bhashyas or the related commentaries. Between Bhamaha and Dandin, critics of the sixth and seventh centuries, and Bhoja, who belonged to the eleventh century, there was a gap of half a millennium; and yet, Bhoja knew their exact critical positions in relation to narrative poetry, sargabandha, or poetic styles, riti. Between Bharata Muni and Abhinavagupta, the gap was of more than six centuries; but Abhinavagupta knew Bharata's formulations on aesthetic emotion to the last detail. It was not just the relationship with his predecessors within the same shastra about which a given thinker was aware; invariably, he was also aware of the relationship between his intellectual or philosophical position and the other related sciences. It is very clear from the text of Abhinavagupta's comments on the shantarasa that he was fully aware that his theoretical position related in various ways to the literary criticism of Ashvagosha, Bharata, Anandavardhana, Bhattatauta, Bhattanayaka, as well as the philosophic positions in Vedanta, *Vijnanabhairava*, *Yogavasistha,* and Kashmir Saivism. On the other hand, Abhinavagupta, in *Gitarthasangraha*, his commentary on the Gita, leaves us in no doubt regarding the line of philosophers and critics to whom he alludes, and who included Katyayana, Saushuka, Bhutiraja, Bhattenduraja, Kallata, Mukula, Somananda, Utpaldeva, Lakshamanagupta, and many other scholars.[26]

In the Sanskrit tradition of philosophic or critical commentaries, textual evidence, oral or written, was considered of great importance. Even when critics made some original observation, they tried to establish its validity by quoting a multitude of verses in support from the available literature, written by predecessors as well as their contemporaries. Modern scholarship of Sanskrit texts has often found that whereas the verses quoted were accurate, there was usually no mention of the name of the author quoted. In any text on poetics,

---

[26] Abhinavagupta, *The Gītārthasangraha*, Abhinav Sharma (trans.), Leiden: E. J. Brill, 1983.

for instance, one finds citations from other poets running into hundreds; but the acknowledgment of authorship is rare. This was not so because the writers in Sanskrit had no sense of history. To be seen as ahistorical had a greater prestige in the value system of the Sanskrit language universe.

The creative writing in Sanskrit composed primarily for aesthetic pleasure developed a large variety of genres and forms. It included works written in verse, prose, and narrative or dramatic forms. It was seen as non-perishable, the akshara canon, and was fairly well-defined during the later centuries of classical literature. It included works by Shudraka (third century CE), Vishakhadatta (fourth century CE), Kalidasa (fourth to fifth centuries CE), Bhartrihari (fifth century CE), Kumaradasa (sixth century CE), Bharavi (sixth century CE), Banabhatta (seventh century CE), Bhatti (seventh century CE), Magha (seventh century CE), Dandin (seventh to eighth centuries CE), Subandhu (seventh century CE), Bhavabhuti (eighth century CE), and Bhattanayaka (ninth century CE). After the eighth century, the volume of compositions expanded. They became stylistically more rigid and thematically less complex. The community of literates declined, giving rise to excessive and often pointless advancement in theoretical literature. And the canon lost its purpose as well as real social importance.

Between the fifth century BCE and the tenth century CE, literary and philosophical works were preserved by reproducing manuscript copies from time to time. These copies were made by teachers in schools and universities, more particularly those living in residential institutions.[27] Maharashtri Prakrit and Sanskrit poet, dramatist, and critic Rajashekhara (tenth century CE) describes a normal day in the life of an acharya–poet. In this description, Rajashekhara records that poets wrote every day for a certain number of hours. Poetry and linguistic compositions in other forms were perceived during the post-Vedic period of Sanskrit literature as essentially written forms. The manuscript copies at schools and centres of learning were used by scholars being trained in the shastras and kavyas. Often, scholars from other centres visited these institutions as part of their nationwide pilgrimage and brought information

---

[27] R. K. Mookherjee, *Ancient Indian Education*, London: Macmillan and Co., 1947.

with them about new compositions or older, lesser-known works. Thus, through the networks of places of pilgrimage and the residential schools, literary manuscripts were replicated and preserved. This method was in use till the beginning of the thirteenth century when paper replaced the traditional materials used for writing manuscripts.

Initially, the shastras made no claim to authority. But their place in the education system inevitably brought an association of authority with them in the course of time. When we compare the texts of philosophic treatises from the time of Panini with those in the age of Shankara (eighth century CE), periods separated by about thirteen centuries, we find that the later texts have no hesitation in claiming direct lineage from the Vedas. The later shastras share with the Vedas their authority, a consequence of the institutionalized teaching of the shastras. It was also the consequence of the hegemony of Sanskrit which pervaded the Indian continent and Southeast Asia.

Bharata Muni, the earliest literary critic, gives us the impression that he comes at the end of a long line of theorists, and that he is presenting a mere summary of their work, but there appears to be no textual evidence to support his statement. That is exactly what happens with Panini's grammar. That is also the case with Chanakya's *Arthashastra*. As a matter of historical fact, there is no major literary or philosophical 'lost' period between the composition of the Vedic anthologies (samhitas) and a settled text of the Mahabharata, on the one hand, and Panini, Patanjali, and Bharata, on the other hand. One has to conclude, therefore, that the cultural practice of assigning an older date of origin to the shastra texts than their actual date of composition was aimed at enhancing their authority.[28]

This was possible because the organizing criterion for the shastras was not 'period' but 'school of thought'. Every text was given a very definite place in terms of the school of philosophy or thought it postulated or explained. The chronological placement of a text was given secondary importance, and it was subsumed within the category of 'school'. In contrast, the akshara literature was accorded the status of 'undiminishing youth'. The

[28] Madhav Deshpande, 'History, Change and Permanence: A Classical Indian Perspective', *Contributions to South Asian Studies*, Vol. 1, Gopal Krishna (ed.), New Delhi: Oxford University Press, 1979, pp. 1–28.

mythological Kavyapurusha was but a youthful child. There are numerous references to the capacity of poetry to remain 'ever-charming' in discussions of alamkara and vakrokti, poetic language. (Some claimed that it was alamkara or embellished language that made poetry, others said that all poetry was vakrokti or indirect/ suggestive language.) Akshara meant non-diminishing, just as it meant 'letters'. When Bhavabhuti hoped that perhaps his poetry would be appreciated by the right kind of readers a thousand years later—

> Utpasyate mama toh koapi samanadharma
> Kalohyaya niraba dhirvipula cha Prithvi
>
> (The earth is vast and Time is infinite; somebody
> on this earth shall there be who will understand
> my verse.)

In saying this, he was voicing the received notions of the everlasting immediacy of akshara literature. For ancient Indian readers, all akshara literature belonged to the 'adyatan' past.

Building upon the creative works of the first millennium, the writers of the second millennium produced a large number of anthologies, despite the fact that most of the Prakrits had managed to stage a comeback and were emerging in the form of various modern Indian languages such as Marathi, Gujarati, Bangla, Odia, Kashmiri, Punjabi, and Sindhi. However, the literature in Sanskrit during the second millennium had clearly lost its vitality. It also kept losing its social relevance. As the Bhakti period literature in modern Indian languages—both the Dravidic and the Indo-Aryan—kept challenging the varna system of social segregation and the associated ideas of pollution, the hegemony of Sanskrit started weakening. Historian Daud Ali points out that 'the trend in the second millennium was toward large compendia comprising verses by many authors organized under an increasingly standard set of diverse topics'.[29] The most prominent among these included the *Subhashitaratnakosha* of Vidyakara (c. 1105), the *Saduktikarnamrita* of Shridharadasa (c. 1205), the *Suktimuktavali* of Bhagadatta Jalhana (c. 1258), the *Shringadharapaddhati* of Shringadhara (c. 1353), and the *Subhashitavali* of Vallabhadeva (after the fifteenth century).

---

[29] Daud, 'Verses at the Court of the King'.

Historically, Sanskrit was not the earliest language of India. When it reached India, it was one of the languages the Indians of that remote past were using. But Sanskrit was the first language to have developed literature and to keep its records alive forever, orally. It was the first language in the world to have produced vastly symbolic literature of extraordinary mystical power. It built an amazing mnemonic enabling generations to access its very first poetic opus, the Rig Veda. Its world view provided the basis of a social order—though legitimizing severe discrimination—which brought almost the entire society of the subcontinent within its fold. Sanskrit, with an extraordinary precision of poetic meters, became a language which carried within it an expansive mythos and mesmerized people for several millennia with its charm. It came to be the principal language of India's rituals and sacred transactions. Its compact aphorisms provided Indians well-coined ideals and goals of life. The scriptures in it, to a very large extent, made India an inward-looking civilization. Most importantly, Sanskrit became the subcontinent's language of esteem, leading hundreds of generations of non-Sanskrit speakers to aspire to 'Sanskritize' themselves. During the twentieth century, the term was used by the sociologist M. N. Srinivas to anchor a theory of social aspiration born out of severe inequalities. Sanskrit provided millions of words and word roots to all other Indian languages. Finally, Sanskrit became the world's most spectacular example of how a language which is not large in its social spread can yet be a language enjoying an exceptionally high esteem. Sanskrit was and continues to be so, despite its decline a thousand years ago, the ultimate language hegemony that the world has seen, no matter if it was not spoken during the Indus era and no matter if it came to India from somewhere else. The history of Indianization of Sanskrit is synonymous with the history of Sanskritization of India, an intimate mutual engagement that Persian and English, too, were to achieve in later ages, but not so pervasively as Sanskrit did.

# BIBLIOGRAPHY

Abhinavagupta, *The Gītārthasangraha*, Abhinav Sharma (trans.), Leiden: E. J. Brill, 1983.

Ali, Daud, 'Verses at the Court of the King: Shifts in the Historical Imagination of the Sanskrit Literary Tradition during the Second Millennium', *Journal of the Royal Asiatic Society*, Series 3, No. 3, January 2022, pp. 13–31.

Anthony, David W., *The Horse, the Wheel, and Language*, Princeton: Princeton University Press, 2007.

Aurobindo, Sri, *The Secret of the Veda*, Pondicherry: Sri Aurobindo Ashram Publication Department, 2012.

Ballantyne, James R., *The Laghu Kaumudi: A Sanskrit Grammar*, 4th edition, Varanasi: E. J. Lazarus & Co., 1849.

Belvalkar, Shripad Krishna, *An Account of the Different Existing Systems of Sanskrit Grammar*, New Delhi: Bharatiya Book Corporation, 1976.

Bhandarkar, Ramkrishna Gopal, *First Book of Sanskrit: Being an Elementary Treatise on Grammar with Exercises*,

Mumbai: Karnataka Publishing House, 1971.

Bhat, G. K., *Bharata-Natya-Manjiri: Bharata on the Theory and Practice of Drama*, Pune: Bhandarkar Oriental Research Institute, 1975.

Bhatt, G. H. (ed.), *The Bālakāṇḍa: The First Book of the Vālmīki Rāmāyaṇa, The National Epic of India*, Vadodara: Oriental Institute, 1960.

Burrow, Thomas, *The Sanskrit Language*, London: Faber and Faber, 1945.

Daniels, Peter T. and Bright, William (eds.), *The World's Writing Systems*, Oxford: Oxford University Press, 1996.

Derrett, J. Duncan M, *Dharmaśāstra and Juridical Literature, A History of Indian Literature*, Vol. 5, Fasc. 1, Jan Gonda (ed.), Wiesbaden: Otto Harrassowitz, 1973.

Deshpande, C. R., *Transmission of the Mahābhārata Tradition: Vyāsa and Vyāsīds*, Shimla: Indian Institute of Advanced Studies, 1978.

Deshpande, Madhav, 'History, Change and Permanence: A Classical Indian Perspective', *Contributions to South Asian Studies*, Vol. 1, Gopal Krishna (ed.), New Delhi: Oxford University Press, 1979, pp.1–28.

Deutsch, Eliot and van Buitenen, J. A. B. (eds.), *A Source Book of Advaita Vedānta*, Honolulu: The University Press of Hawaii, 1971.

Devy, G. N., '*Of Many Heroes*': *An Indian Essay in Literary Historiography*, Hyderabad: Orient Blackswan, 1999.

Dyson, Tim, *A Population History of India: From the First Modern People to the Present Day*, Oxford: Oxford University Press, 2018.

Elizarenkova, T. J., *Language and Style of the Vedic Ṛṣis*, Wendy Doniger (ed.), New York: State University of New York Press, 1995.

Gebow, Edwin, *Indian Poetics, A History of Indian Literature*, Vol. 5, Fasc. 3, Jan Gonda (ed.), Wiesbaden: Otto Harrassowitz, 1977.

Gonda, Jan, *Medieval Religious Literature in Sanskrit, A History of Indian Literature*, Vol. 2, Fasc. 1, Wiesbaden: Otto Harrassowitz, 1977.

Gonda, Jan, *The Ritual Sūtras, A History of Indian Literature*, Vol. 1, Fasc. 2, Wiesbaden: Otto Harrassowitz, 1977.

Griffith, Ralph T. H. and Keith, Arthur Berriedale (trans.), *The Vedas: The Samhitās of the Rig, Yajur (White and Black), Sama, and Atharva*, Jon William Fergus (ed.), CreateSpace Independent Publishing Platform, 2017.

Haak, W., Lazaridis I., Patterson, N., et al., 'Massive migration from the steppe was a source for Indo-European languages in Europe', *Nature*, No. 522, 2015, pp. 207–11.

Hart, George Luzerne, *The Relation Between Tamil and*

*Classical Sanskrit Literature, A History of Indian Literature*, Vol. 10, Fasc. 2, Jan Gonda (ed.), Wiesbaden: Otto Harrassowitz, 1976.

Hudson, Dennis, 'The Responses of Tamils to Their Study by Westerners 1608-1908', *Comparative Civilizations Review*, Vol. 13, No. 13, Article 14, 1985.

Jones, Sir William, 'The Third Anniversary Discourse, on the Hindus'. Delivered on 2 February 1986. Printed in Sir William Jones, *Works*, Vol. 1, pp. 19–34. Reproduced in Winfred P. Lehmann (ed.), *Nineteenth Century Historical Indo-European Linguistics*, London and Bloomington: Indiana University Press, 1967.

Karve, Irawati, *Yuganta: The End of an Epoch*, New Delhi: Sangam Books, 1974.

Krishnamoorthy, K. (ed. and trans.), *Ānandavardhana's Dhvanyāloka*, Dharwad: Karnataka University Press, 1974.

Krishnamoorthy, K. (ed. and trans.), *The Vakrokti-jīvita of Kuntaka*, Dharwad: Karnataka University Press, 1977.

Lazaridis, Iosif, Nadel, Dani, Rohland, Nadin, et al., 'Genomic Insights into the origin of farming in the ancient Near East' , *Nature*, No. 536, 2016, pp. 419–24.

Lazaridis, Iosif, Patterson, Nick, Anthony, David, et al.,'The genetic origin of the Indo-Europeans', *Nature*, No. 639, February 2025.

Lienhard, Siegfried, *A History of Classical Poetry: Sanskrit-Pali-Prakrit, A History of Indian Literature*, Vol. 3, Fasc. 1, Jan Gonda (ed.), Wiesbaden: Otto Harrassowitz, 1984.

Masica, Colin P., *The Indo-Aryan Languages*, Cambridge: Cambridge University Press, 1991.

Masson, J. L. and Patwardhan, M. V., *Śāntarasa and Abhinavagupta's Philosophy of Aesthetics*, Bhandarkar Oriental Series, No. 9, Pune: Bhandarkar Oriental Research Institute, 1969.

Matilal, Bimal Krishna, *The Word and the World: India's Contribution to the Study of Language*, Delhi and New York: Oxford University Press. 1990.

Mookerji, Radha Kumud, *Ancient Indian Education (Brahmanical and Buddhist)*, London: Macmillan and Co., 1947.

Muller, Max, *A History of Ancient Sanskrit Literature*, London: Williams and Norgate, 1860.

Nath, R. and Faiyaz 'Gwaliari', *India As Seen by Amir Khusrau (in 1318 A.D.)*, Jaipur: Historical Documentation Programme, 1981.

Nijenhuis, E., *Musicological Literature, A History of Indian Literature*, Vol. 6, Fasc. 1, Jan Gonda (ed.), Wiesbaden: Otto Harrassowitz, 1977.

Norman, K. R., *Pāli literature: including the canonical literature in Prakrit and Sanskrit of all the Hīnayāna schools of Buddhism*, Vol. 7, Fasc. 2, Jan Gonda (ed.), Wiesbaden: Otto Harrassowitz, 1983.

Ollett, Andrew, 'Early inscriptions', in G. N. Devy, Tony Joseph, and Ravi Korisettar (eds.), *The Indians: Histories of a Civilization*, New Delhi: Aleph Book Company, 2023.

Pillai, K. Raghavan, *The Vākyapadīya: Critical Text of Cantos I and II*, New Delhi: Motilal Banarsidass, 1971.

Pollock, Sheldon, *The Language of the Gods in the World of Men: Sanskrit, Culture, and Power in Premodern India*, Los Angeles: University of California Press, 2006.

Rajan, K., *Early Writing System: A Journey from Graffiti to Brahmi*, Madurai: Pandya Nadu Centre for Archaeological Research, 2015.

Reich, David, *Who We Are and How We Got Here*, Oxford: Oxford University Press, 2018.

Robinson, Andrew, *Lost Languages: The Enigma of the Undeciphered Scripts*, New York: McGraw-Hill, 2002.

Rocher, Ludo, *The Purāṇas, A History of Indian Literature*, Vol. 2, Fasc. 3, Jan Gonda (ed.), Wiesbaden: Otto Harrassowitz, 1986.

Sastri Siromani, K. S. Ramaswami (ed.), *Kāvyamīmāṃsā of Rājaśekhara*, Vadodara: Oriental Institute, 1934.

Savarkar, V. D., 'Some of the Basic Principles and Tenets of the Hindu Movement', *Hindu Rashtra Darshan*, Bombay: Savarkar Prakashan, 1984.

Scharfb, Hartmut, *Grammatical Literature, A History of Indian Literature*, Vol. 5, Fasc. 2, Jan Gonda (ed.), Wiesbaden: Otto Harrassowitz, 1977.

Singer, Milton, *When a Great Tradition Modernizes: An Anthropological Approach to Indian Civilization*, New York: Praeger Publishers, 1972.

Singh, Jaideva (trans.), *The Doctrine of Recognition: A Translation of Pratyabhijñāhrdayam*, New York: State University of New York Press, 1990.

Spinney, Laura, *Proto: How One Ancient Language Went Global*, London: William Collins, 2025.

Staal, J. F. (ed.), *A Reader on the Sanskrit Grammarians*, Cambridge: The MIT Press, 1972.

Staal, F. (ed.), *Agni: The Vedic Ritual of the Fire Altar*, Berkley: Asian Humanities Press, 1983.

Staal, F., *Discovering the Vedas: Origins, Mantras, Rituals, Insights*, New Delhi: Penguin India, 2008.

Sternbach, Ludwik, *Subhāsita, Gnomic and Didactic Literature, A History of Indian Literature*, Vol. 4, Fasc. 1, Jan Gonda (ed.), Wiesbaden: Otto Harrassowitz, 1974.

Sukthankar, Vishnu S. (ed.), *The Mahābhārata*, Pune: Bhandarkar Oriental Research Institute, 1925–1943.

Trautmann, Thomas R. (ed.), *The Aryan Debate: Debates in Indian History and Society*, New Delhi: Oxford University Press, 2007.

Vaidya, C. V., *History of Sanskrit Literature, Vol. 1—Sruti (Vedic) Period*, Pune: Aryabhushan Press, 1930.

Vogel, Claus, *Indian Lexicography, A History of Indian Literature*, Vol. 5, Fasc. 4, Jan Gonda (ed.), Wiesbaden: Otto Harrassowitz, 1979.

Walimbe, S. R., 'Aryan Invasion in the Indian subcontinent: Facts and Fallacies The Physical Anthropological Perspective', *Iranian Journal of Archaeological* Studies, Vol. 1, No. 1, 2011.

Whitney, William Dwight, *History of Sanskrit Grammar*, New Delhi: Sanjay Prakashan, 2002.

Woolner, A. C., *Introduction to Prakrit*, Varanasi: R. S. Panna Lal & Co., 1917.

www.ingramcontent.com/pod-product-compliance
Lightning Source LLC
Chambersburg PA
CBHW020441100426
42812CB00036B/3404/J